D1713489

Photo by Cliff Moore

A scene from the McCarter Theatre Company production of "The Day They Shot John Lennon." Set design by Daniel Boylen.

THE DAY THEY SHOT

JOHN LENNON

by

JAMES McLURE

DRAMATISTS
PLAY SERVICE
INC.

SPECIAL NOTE ON SONGS AND RECORDINGS

For performance of such songs and recordings mentioned in this play as are in copyright, the permission of the copyright owners must be obtained; or other songs and recordings in the public domain substituted.

THE DAY THEY SHOT JOHN LENNON was first presented by the McCarter Theatre Company, in Princeton, New Jersey, in January, 1983. It was directed by Robert Lanchester; the scenery was by Daniel Boylen; costumes were by Susan Rheaume; and the lighting was by Richard Moore. The cast, in order of appearance, was as follows:

FRAN . . . . Mercedes Ruehl
SALLY . . . . Ann Adams
KEVIN. . . . . Greg Thornton
MIKE. . . . . Clifford Fetters
LARRY . . . . Damien Leake
MORRIS. . . . . .Karl Light
SILVIO. . . . . .Tony Campisi
GATELY . . . . Gregory Grove
BRIAN. . . . . .Gary Roberts

SCENE

Across the street from the Dakota apartment building, 72nd Street and Central Park West, New York City. There is a light mist falling.

TIME

December 9, 1980

CHARACTERS

FRAN LOWENSTEIN 35, a native New Yorker and all that that implies. Tough, sensitive, a feminist and a member of the Woodstock generation who is also looking for "a meaningful relationship."

BRIAN MURPHY 33, in Advertising. Though given to quick opinions and stances of self-confidence he is basically a confused individual looking for love.

SALLY 16, like all the white kids in the play she is very middle-class. Her heart is also breaking for the first time.

KEVIN 16, Sally's ex-boyfriend. Cocky, self-assured and slightly macho. Has never had his heart broken.

MIKE 16, sensitive, intelligent young man. His heart is broken all the time. He'll become either a priest, a poet, or an embittered liberal.

MORRIS 70's, an elderly widower, lived in the neighborhood all his life. Alternately belligerent, confused, guarded. A very lonely old man who would resent being called old.

LARRY 18, an urban black kid. His street-wise arrogance and irony masks a strong intelligence and sensitivity.

SILVIO An embittered Veteran of the Viet Nam war. Street-wise, tough and in a way still at war.

GATELY Silvio's friend and also a Vet. Unlike Silvio however, Gately has not adapted to the mental pressures of civilian life. Both spent considerable time in V.A. hospitals for physical and psychological wounds. Both are currently unemployed.

THE DAY THEY SHOT
JOHN LENNON

FRAN. I woke up that morning and thought — something's wrong . . . something's really wrong. Then I remembered. It was like that song: "I heard the news today — Oh boy." (*Pause.*)

SALLY. I was doing my homework. I had a lot that night. I had a lot of geometry, I remember, and that's not my best subject anyway. I mean, I'm terrible at it if you want to know the truth. And I heard it on my T.V. you know? I had it down real low, 'cause my mom doesn't like me to play it when I'm doing my homework 'cause she says I can't concentrate. But I can. T.V. relaxes me. And then I heard the news vaguely in the background. And it didn't seem real. Maybe because it was T.V. I mean it was *realistic*, y'know, but it didn't seem *real*. I wanted to talk to Kevin, to talk to Kevin, to talk to someone to make it seem real. Kevin's my boyfriend. I mean, he used to be but then we broke up. It's a *long* story. Anyway I wanted to call Kevin and talk to him to express something, to make it *real*, because I had to make sense out of it, and I knew Kevin would understand. Kevin's very intense. Anyway my mother told me it was too late and I couldn't call him, and so I had to go to bed. (*Pause.*)

KEVIN. My friend Mikey called me and I couldn't believe it. He heard it and just went to pieces. And I tried to talk to him but he was crying and everything. Sometimes people depend on me 'cause I guess I'm mature for my age, or I don't know . . . just . . . sensitive I guess. Anyway we all decided to skip classes the next day and meet in the city. Mikey and me and Sally. Sally's my ex-girlfriend but it's cool. We've agreed to stay good friends. (*Pause.*)

MIKE. I was hysterical. I couldn't talk hardly to anyone. It didn't seem like anybody would ever understand me ever again. My father came into my room and told me to quit crying. He said it was stupid to cry over a musician. (*Pause.*)

LARRY. I was like hanging out, y'know, getting a little high and somebody comes up an' says, "Hey man, you heard what happened?" I said, "Naw man, heard what?" And he said "Man, you mean you ain't heard?" And I said "Naw man, I just got through tellin' you I ain't heard nothing", and he said "You mean you really ain't heard?" I said "Shit man, you jiving me. Now get on outta here." Dude left, man. (*Pause.*) An' I had to find out what was happenin'. Cause when the real bad shit starts comin down, you don't wanna be the last to know, y'know. (*Pause.*)

MORRIS. I missed the whole thing. Fell asleep watching the late movie. Good movie too. Something with Barbara Stanwyck. When she was young, she was a little honey, let me tell you. But I fell asleep. What're you gonna do. (*Pause.*) Did you hear she got mugged? Barbara Stanwyck. Yeah, they broke into her house. Beverly Hills. All that money and no security. The world is a dangerous place. (*Pause.*) Yessir, when she was young, she was a little honey. She was in this movie. What was it? Oh, *you* know, the one I mean. It was when she was a dance hall girl and they sang:

"Honolulu Baby, where'd you get those eyes
and your dark complexion — that I idolize.
Honolulu Baby, where'd you get those eyes?"*

(*Pause.*) I take it back. It wasn't Barbara Stanwyck. It was Laurel and Hardy.

SILVIO. We were selling dope down at St. Mark's Place, and I don't really care what you think about that. I gave up carin' about what people like you think about people like us the day we came back from Nam. Oh, by the way, thanks for the

---

*See Special Note on copyright page.

ticker tape parade. Really nice. So when I heard about it, I just shook my head, man. 'Cause I know who was responsible and why. It's only people like us who understood the whole thing. (*Pause.*) You don't even understand that much, do you?

GATELY. Shit. I ain't understood nothing since 1969. (*Pause.*)

BRIAN. I just had to be there in the crowd. I mean I knew that's where I had to be. And that surprised me. Not because I didn't care, because I did. But—I mean, look, I'm not an emotional guy. I mean I'm sensitive, but I'm not overly sensitive. The only time I really cried was when my mother died. But when you walked down Columbus Avenue, you saw it on everyone's faces. In their eyes. We were all thinking the same thing. I was on my way to work and suddenly I felt myself walking there, y'know, to where it happened, almost by instinct. I wanted to be part of the crowd . . . Y'know it's funny . . . the feeling of the crowd wasn't completely one of . . . mourning. It was sad at times. It also felt good at times . . . sometimes people would start singing one of the songs . . . all those songs . . . Sure, some people were crying. But there was also a feeling of belonging. Or paying respect or witnessing . . . Yeah, we were witnessing. Yeah, the crowd was something. (*Pause.*)

FRAN. I woke up that morning and thought—something's wrong . . . something's really wrong. Then I remembered . . . it's like the song: I heard the news today—Oh Boy."

(*The actors begin to move into their respective tableaux. Silvio and Gately come forward.*)

SILVIO. Look at 'em all. They don't even know what they're doing here. Something like this happens and it really shakes 'em up. God, I hate civilians.

GATELY. (*Pause.*) Silvio, wait.

SILVIO. What for . ?

GATELY. Are you sure we're gonna do this?

SILVIO. Sure I'm sure, why?

GATELY. Well, I'm not so sure.

9

SILVIO. What's the matter?

GATELY. I'm a little nervous.

SILVIO. It's natural.

GATELY. My hands are shakin'.

SILVIO. They'll quit after the first one.

GATELY. And Silvio . . .

SILVIO. What?

GATELY. I may pee in my pants.

SILVIO. C'mere, what's the matter with you? You're acting like you don't know the score. You were in Nam right?

GATELY. Right.

SILVIO. You got shot at, right?

GATELY. I not only got shot *at*, I got shot *up*.

SILVIO. Precisely my point. You've seen some heavy shit, my friend. We know what it's all about. We've eaten the fuckin' reality sandwich. Every grunt in Nam knows something these people don't know. We've walked with kings. Never forget that. These people here are different. They've never encountered death. They're just civilians. They're like cows. Look at 'em. Last night someone was killed and it knocks 'em all out of their snug little cocoons. They don't even know what they're doing here. They don't know.

GATELY. But we know?

SILVIO. Right. Shit if it hadn't been for Nam we'd be like all these other assholes. Right?

GATELY. . . . Right. (*Mike and Kevin step forward.*)

MIKE. What're you gonna do?

KEVIN. There's nothing to do.

MIKE. Where are the words.

KEVIN. There are no words.

MIKE. I mean, is the whole world going crazy or is it just me?

KEVIN. It's not just you, Mikey.

MIKE. So it *is* the whole world?

KEVIN. The whole world what?

MIKE. That's going crazy.

KEVIN. I tell you Mikey, I just don't know.

MIKE. I mean they got the bomb. They got people starving all over the world, they got the war in the Middle East. Kevin, I may lose it.

KEVIN. You got Northern Ireland.

MIKE. Oh man, I can't handle Northern Ireland. I don't understand it at all. I mean, they're both Irish.

KEVIN. And now this.

MIKE. And now this. I don't know. I got all this hurt inside me. All this grief inside, ya know. Right here. And it hurts, man, it hurts.

KEVIN. Do you feel like you want to talk about it?

MIKE. I feel like I want to talk about it, but I don't know if I'll say the right thing.

KEVIN. Just say what's human and it'll be the right thing.

MIKE. Wow . . . that's heavy.

KEVIN. I know.

MIKE. Kevin?

KEVIN. What?

MIKE. I gotta talk about it.

KEVIN. Mikey.

MIKE. What?

KEVIN. You gotta do what you gotta do. If you gotta talk — talk. (*Silence.*) I thought you were gonna talk.

MIKE. I'm mustering my thoughts.

KEVIN. Well, don't take all day.

MIKE. Huh?

KEVIN. This sort of thing has to be spontaneous. Just let her rip.

MIKE. (*Rapidly.*) I don't know, just all these thoughts, all these old impressions, to me he was like, a saint, a saint; I mean he taught us a lot about love. I mean most people teach death but he *loved*, he loved his wife and his son and even though in the early days he was fucked up a lot, a lot, and dropping acid, I mean isn't that just like any great artist who feels the pain for all of us? Isn't it? Isn't it?

KEVIN. Yeah! Keep going. You're on a roll!

MIKE. I don't know where all this is comin' from but y'know

11

it's like, it's pourin' out y'know.

KEVIN. Let it pour! It's human, for Chrissakes.

MIKE. He was like Christ. He was a seeker for truth. He was like always trying to find the truth underneath the bullshit. It was like, remember in parochial school when they told us that when Christ was a kid that he was always runnin' off from mass and talkin' to the holy men and the holy men didn't get it 'cause they were all hung up in a lot of religious details, and they couldn't see where Christ was comin' from 'cause he was always looking out for the truth. Well, John was like that. When, y'know, they went to the Maharishi and they all thought the Maharishi was a good guy and all and then they found out that he was full of shit and when they were leaving him, the Maharishi said, "Why are you leaving me?" and John said—"You know, if you're so smart and mystical and everything, you oughta be able to figure it out for yourself." I mean the guy that says that is a seeker for the truth. God. (*Pause.*) I mean, I've been listening to this man's music all my life. Ever since 1975.

KEVIN. You know what I want you to do for me?

MIKE. What?

KEVIN. When Sally gets here, I want you to repeat word for word to her what you just said to me.

MIKE. I just spoke from the heart.

KEVIN. I never seen you so colloquial. (*Fran and Brian come forward.*)

BRIAN. Unbelievable.

FRAN. Disgusting.

BRIAN. Can you believe this?

FRAN. It's unbelievable.

BRIAN. I can't believe it.

FRAN. What has our society come to? Now we're shooting our artists. People we need. Our brightest talents. I mean, if someone's going to change the world, it's going to be an artist, not a politician. I mean, the man's only fault was to tell us about love. Is love that dangerous? The man wrote songs, for God's sake. He was trying to live a decent life. I mean the

12

Beatles *were* the sixties! They changed the world! They taught us love—"Love is all you need."

BRIAN. Say, were you at Woodstock?

FRAN. Yeah. How'd you know?

BRIAN. I was at Woodstock too!

FRAN. Were you?

BRIAN. Yeah! Isn't that incredible.

FRAN. What a coincidence.

BRIAN. It's incredible! What a coincidence?

FRAN. I mean, how many people were at Woodstock?

BRIAN. Oh, about five hundred thousand. (*Pause.*) Cigarette?

FRAN. I gave it up.

BRIAN. Good for you.

FRAN. It's a disgusting habit.

BRIAN. I know.

FRAN. It gives you cancer.

BRIAN. I know.

FRAN. I mean, how long does it take for people to wake up?

BRIAN. I know. How long's it been since you quit?

FRAN. Yesterday.

BRIAN. Well, still it's good that you stuck with it.

FRAN. Aw, what the hell, Gimme one. (*They smoke.*) Thanks.

BRIAN. I mean, in my opinion, there's no other composer of the twentieth century that can compare with Lennon. No way. (*Pause.*) Name me one. (*Pause.*)

FRAN. Well, Gershwin was good.

BRIAN. Sure he was. Sure he was. But he didn't have the effect that Lennon did.

FRAN. Well, of course not. You couldn't be more correct. But Gershwin wrote a lot of great tunes.

BRIAN. Well. Goes without saying. But that's not my point.

FRAN. "A Foggy Day in London Town" is one of my favorite songs.

BRIAN. O yeah, sure, terrific tune. I got an Ella Fitzgerald album that's got a terrific rendition of "Foggy Day."

FRAN. I love Ella. She's the best.

BRIAN. But my point about the Beatles, is that nobody, no group, no individual, no artist of any kind has ever created that kind of phenomenon before, or effected society in such a massive way. (*Pause.*) That's my point about the Beatles.

FRAN. (*Slightly irked.*) I got your point. Right away I got your point.

BRIAN. Good. (*Pause.*) I just didn't want you to miss my point.

FRAN. Unbelievable.

BRIAN. Yeah, I couldn't go to work today.

FRAN. Me either. I said to hell with it and walked right through the park.

BRIAN. Oh, you live on the east side?

FRAN. Yeah. I couldn't face work.

BRIAN. Where do you work?

FRAN. In a law firm.

BRIAN. You're a lawyer? That's fantastic.

FRAN. Not really. I'm a secretary.

BRIAN. Well, that's nice too.

FRAN. Yeah, but it's not fantastic. I have a B.F.A.

BRIAN. Me, I'm in advertising.

FRAN. Are you?

BRIAN. Yeah . . . uh, Brian Murphy.

FRAN. Uh, Fran Lowenstein. (*They shake.*) Hmpf.

BRIAN. What?

FRAN. You're in advertising and I'm a secretary on Madison Avenue.

BRIAN. So?

FRAN. We were both at Woodstock.

BRIAN. . . . Yeah. (*They face forward.*) It's unbelievable.

FRAN. It's disgustin. (*Pause. They recede. Larry moves D. Larry's a black guy, early twenties. He carries a large portable radio, blaring "I Wanna Hold Your Hand."* Simultaneously*

*See Special Note on copyright page.

from another part of the stage, moves Morris, a man in his late 70's. He walks with a cane. They cross and bump into each other. Morris falls down.)

LARRY. Hey, man, watch where you're going.

MORRIS. What?

LARRY. I said watch it.

MORRIS. What? *(Larry turns down radio.)*

LARRY. I said watch it.

MORRIS. Watch it! How can I watch it? I'm being run over. Help me up! Help me!

LARRY. Jesus *(Larry helps him up. Morris stands, dusts himself off. Then hits Larry feebly with his cane.)* Shit, man, what's the matter with you?

MORRIS. That's what's wrong with the world today. No respect for the elderly.

LARRY. I got news for you. You ain't elderly no more. You're old. Pure "D" old.

MORRIS. No respect. *(Morris raises cane again feebly.)*

LARRY. Shit man. How you're gonna get any respect if you're all the time fixin' to hit somebody with a stick? *(Morris grudgingly lowers cane. Grumbles darkly. Regards crowd.)*

MORRIS. *(Grouchily.)* Why the hell are all these people here?

LARRY. Shit. Where you been man Mars?

MORRIS. *(Pointing.)* I've lived in that building for thirty-five years. Don't you tell me about this neighborhood.

LARRY. Man. Don't you know last night John Lennon was shot?

MORRIS. Who?

LARRY. John Lennon.

MORRIS. Oh. *(Pause.)* Who's John Lennon?

LARRY. *(Irate high voice.)* Who's John Lennon? Who's John Lennon?! Aw, forget it, man! Just forget it! Move to Miami.

MORRIS. I don't like Miami. I've got a sister in Miami.

LARRY. Yeah, and I know what she's doing there, too.

MORRIS. What?

LARRY. Stayin' away from *you*. *(Pause.)*

15

MORRIS. I know who he was now. They shot him?

LARRY. Yeah. Right over there.

MORRIS. That's what's wrong with the country today. You're not safe to walk the streets. They shoot you. (*Pause.*) Terrible times. Terrible. I saw him on T.V. just the other night. He was a very funny man. It was a movie with Shirley MacLaine.

LARRY. What?

MORRIS. She's a dancer you know. Very talented. She went to China.

LARRY. Who are you talking about?

MORRIS. Shirley MacLaine.

LARRY. Aw, give it up, old man.

MORRIS. He was very good in that one where he played the alcoholic, too.

LARRY. Who was?

MORRIS. Jack Lemmon.

LARRY. Aw, give me a break, fuzz head.

MORRIS. (*Pause.*) Why would anybody want to shoot Jack Lemmon? (*Pause.*) Terrible times. (*Mike and Kevin move forward.*)

MIKE. Is Sally coming?

KEVIN. Yeah, I called her.

MIKE. I thought you two weren't speaking.

KEVIN. We're not.

MIKE. I thought you two broke up because of Rhoda Fahrquhar.

KEVIN. We did.

MIKE. But you're speaking now.

KEVIN. Just for today Mikey. This is a very special day. If I know Sally—and I do—she's going to be all upset. I mean I'm upset and I'm a guy.

MIKE. I'm a guy and I'm upset.

KEVIN. Sure you are Mikey, buy you're a sensitive guy. I mean you read poetry and you auditioned for the school play.

MIKE. But you're sensitive Kevin, otherwise how could we be friends?

KEVIN. I am sensitive. I'm not unsensitive. It's just that I'm less sensitive than you. I mean I'm sensitive but I'm still macho. (*Sally comes in. Joins them. They all hug.*)

SALLY. God! Oh God! This is the worst thing that's ever happened.

MIKE. Sally!

SALLY. Mikey!

KEVIN. Sally.

SALLY. (*Cooler.*) Hello Kevin.

MIKE. God! I'm glad you're here.

SALLY. It's good to see you, Mikey.

KEVIN. He's been very emotionally distraught. I've never seen him like this.

SALLY. Well, some people are very sensitive, Kevin.

KEVIN. It's never gonna be the same.

SALLY. It's so horrible. It's so gross I may drop out of school.

KEVIN. You can't drop out of high school, Sally. Get serious.

SALLY. If I have a mental breakdown I can. And I may, too! I mean, have you heard?

MIKE. Heard what?

SALLY. The latest news.

KEVIN. No, what?

MIKE. I don't want to hear.

SALLY. It's so weird.

MIKE. It's all so weird. (*Pause.*)

SALLY. He was killed by someone from Hawaii.

KEVIN. Hawaii?

MIKE. Hawaii. I don't get it.

SALLY. Precisely, because you never think about a killer coming from Hawaii. I mean, what do you think about when you think about Hawaii?

KEVIN. Surfboards, sandy beaches —

MIKE. Bette Midler.

SALLY. Precisely. you don't think about homicide in Hawaii. I mean, there's "Hawaii 5-0", but you don't think about it.

KEVIN. Hawaii?

17

MIKE. I don't get it. It's like a paradise there. How could you have problems in Hawaii?

SALLY. And that's not all.

KEVIN. So what else?

SALLY. It's unbelievable.

MIKE. Oh shit!

KEVIN. Oh God.

SALLY. You ready?

KEVIN. I'm ready.

MIKE. I think I'm ready.

SALLY. He thought he *was* John.

KEVIN. What!

MIKE. Huh.

SALLY. The guy had freaked out to the point that he identified with John so much that he signed his name as John and he married an oriental woman. I mean John was his favorite Beatle and everything. He loved John.

KEVIN. Loved him?

MIKE. If he loved him — why?

KEVIN. People killing people because they *love* them?

MIKE. The world's gone crazy and they're gonna blow it up before we even had a chance to do it.

KEVIN. To do what?

MIKE. . . . Whatever it is that we were gonna do when we grow up.

SALLY. It's disgusting. He bought this gun for like, y'know, less than $100 or something, without a test or anything to see whether you're crazy. It's like for a hundred dollars you can kill Beethoven.

MIKE. Beethoven was one of the greatest.

KEVIN. But it's classical.

MIKE. But if you got into it, you'd like it.

KEVIN. Maybe if I got into it.

SALLY. Think about it, Kevin: it would take time and commitment.

KEVIN. Beethoven was as good as Mozart.

KEVIN. Only he was German.

SALLY. Weren't they both German?

KEVIN. Huh?

SALLY. I thought they were all German, nearly. All those classical biggies.

KEVIN. Germany produced some of the biggies, but not all of the biggies.

SALLY. I know that Kevin. I didn't say all. Did I say all the biggies were German. I said "nearly."

KEVIN. I didn't hear.

SALLY. Well, next time, listen. (*Fran and Brian step forward.*)

FRAN. How could a country that gave us Beethoven, Brahms, Einstein, Freud, give us Auschwitz and Dachau? How could it have happened? Why did we let it? It's the central question of the century.

BRIAN. I agree.

FRAN. Do you ever think about that?

BRIAN. Sometime, sure.

FRAN. Well, you ought to think about it more. If we could figure *that* out, we could figure out everything.

BRIAN. But we can't figure that out.

FRAN. I know. (*Pause.*) Where was world opinion? No one did anything. Auschwitz, Dachau —

BRIAN. Cambodia.

FRAN. Cambodia. Cambodia? Do you mean, like, the Christmas bombings? You mean in the seventies?

BRIAN. No, I mean like last year. Pol Pot.

FRAN. Oh yeah . . . (*Larry and Morris. Larry's radio is on very loud.*)

MORRIS. Would you mind turning that down?

LARRY. What's the matter? You scared it'll make you deaf?

MORRIS. I'm already partially deaf and I still want you to turn it down. (*Pause. He turns it down. Peering.*) Wait a minute. Don't I know you?

LARRY. No, you don't.

MORRIS. Yes I do!

LARRY. No you don't!

MORRIS. Oh yes I do!

LARRY. I tell you, you don't!

MORRIS. You're Eddie's son. Your father's the door man of my building. Sure, yeah, he talks about you all the time. All the time.

LARRY. Yeah? What does he say?

MORRIS. He says you're a bum. You're hanging around with a bad buncha kids. You're doin' this marijuana thing, runnin' around, listenin' to music, girls, you oughta be ashamed of yourself.

LARRY. Nine million people in the *Naked City* and I gotta bump into you.

MORRIS. You're driving your father crazy. You'll break his heart. You're giving him a heart attack.

LARRY. He's already had a heart attack.

MORRIS. See there? Aren't you ashamed of yourself.

LARRY. Say, can I buy back my introduction to you?

MORRIS. You know, you're the first black kid I've talked to in ten years.

LARRY. Greeaat.

MORRIS. I can see we have a lot to talk about. You're going to have a hard time getting rid of me.

LARRY. Great. (*Silvio and Gately come forward.*)

GATELY. I don't feel right about this, Silvio. I really don't. Can't we just stand around like everybody else?

SILVIO. What's the matter with you?

GATELY. It's just weird. I mean today's the day after he was shot.

SILVIO. Maybe that's what it is to you, but you know what today is to me?

GATELY. What?

SILVIO. Tuesday.

GATELY. . . . I just don't feel like doin' it today.

SILVIO. Y'know that's the difference between me and you. I'm a professional. I go to work even when I don't feel like

20

it. Even when I don't feel my best I show up for work.

GATELY. But picking people's pockets?

SILVIO. (*Shushing.*) Would you shut up? What d'ya wanna do "Advertise."

GATELY. I'm sorry. I wasn't thinkin.

SILVIO. You work with me. You're gonna have to start doin' some thinkin' even though you'll be at a disadvantage since you ain't got a brain.

GATELY. I gotta brain.

SILVIO. Tie your shoe.

GATELY. What?

SILVIO. Tie your shoe. You're gonna fall over your own feet. (*Gately bends to tie tennis shoes.*) (*To God.*) You see what I'm dealing with here? Defective material.

GATELY. It's just that we've never done this before.

SILVIO. Hey! It doesn't mean that we can't. Hey! This is America. You can do anything if you put your mind to it.

GATELY. I don't know. Sellin' dope's one thing . . .

SILVIO. Hey! When was our rent due?

GATELY. Three weeks ago.

SILVIO. Three weeks ago for a filthy cold dump that even the cockroaches won't live in! But even *that* they're gonna kick our ass out of it we don't come up with the rent.

GATELY. Maybe we could—

SILVIO. Maybe we could nothin'. I served my country. I ain't gonna go on welfare. (*Pause.*) Besides this is a perfect set-up. Look at this crowd. Shit. All those rich folks in an emotional state. Their minds are elsewhere. Completely preoccupied. They won't even miss it till they hail a cab. That's the way the whole world works my friend. They distract your attention and then they fuck ya.

GATELY. . . . Who's they?

SILVIO. The government. Banks. Nixon.

GATELY. Yeah?

SILVIO. (*Shrugs.*) Shit yeah. Take the Cambodian bombings.

GATELY. OK.

SILVIO. While everyone's sitting at home, Christmastime, living in their little Norman Rockwell world that's when they bomb the shit outta Cambodia, right? When no one's lookin'.
GATELY. I never thought of that.
SILVIO. Shit yeah. It's all one big conspiracy.
GATELY. You mean like Kennedy?
SILVIO. Yeah, like Kennedy. Like King, like Bobby Kennedy. Like uh . . . Malcolm X. Sure. Look. They let ya have Oswald, and the school book depository, and the grassy knoll, just to keep your wheels spinnin'. It's just like when you hear a noise, right? You look to where that noise is coming from, right?
GATELY. Right.
SILVIO. Bam! Hey! What the shit was that? Right? You look over there, right?
GATELY. Right.
SILVIO. But that ain't looking where you should be lookin'.
GATELY. (*Spooked.*) Where should I be lookin'?
SILVIO. (*Points opposite.*) Over there.
GATELY. Why?
SILVIO. (*Eerily.*) Cause the guys with the guns are walking out the back door. And they don't rush. They could be splattered with blood and bone and they don't rush. They don't rush because they don't have to. And they don't have to cause you don't see 'em.
GATELY. Are they invisible?
SILVIO. Better than that.
GATELY. Why can't I see 'em?
SILVIO. Because. (*Pause.*) They're wearing suits.
GATELY. (*Scared.*) Oh shit.
SILVIO. Not only suits. They got hats . . . ties . . . tie clasps . . . button down collars.
GATELY. Shit . . .
SILVIO. Class rings . . . vests . . . snazzy shoes.
GATELY. Aw shit.
SILVIO. Then you know what they do?
GATELY. What?

SILVIO. They go out in the alley and grab a smoke and chuckle about their days work and talk like guys in offices. Like: "Catch you later, Jack." and — "Don't do anything I wouldn't do." And — "What does your broker say." And then you know what they do?

GATELY. What?

SILVIO. They go home to the suburbs to their wives and their kids and drink their martinis and watch Walter Cronkite.

GATELY. Do they do all that?

SILVIO. They do *all* that . . . The rule of thumb is: No matter what you think you know: it isn't the truth. It's a diversion. The guys with the guns are gettin' out the back even as we speak.

GATELY. . . . How much do they get away with — these guys.

SILVIO. . . . They get away with it all. (*Silence. It sinks into Gately.*)

GATELY. Gee. Kennedy. King. Kennedy.

SILVIO. Saigon.

GATELY. Saigon?

SILVIO. You think we didn't have guys killed in Saigon?

GATELY. (*Pause.*) Kent State?

SILVIO. Kent State. (*Pause.*) Lenny Bruce.

GATELY. What?

SILVIO. Glenn Miller.

GATELY. Huh?

SILVIO. Marilyn Monroe.

GATELY. No.

SILVIO. Elvis.

GATELY. Elvis!?

SILVIO. An now . . . this . . .

GATELY. Shit. I'm scared, Silvio. You're not kiddin'? You're not just kiddin'.

SILVIO. I'm not kiddin'. I was in Saigon.

GATELY. What do we do? Oh shit! What do we *do*?

SILVIO. Nothing.

GATELY. What?

SILVIO. You go back to work. Business as usual.

GATELY. (*Pause.*) Like nothing ever happened?

SILVIO. (*Pause.*) Oooblah-di. Oooblah-dah. (*They move U. Silvio and Gately begin moving through the crowd, obviously checking them out. Fran and Brian come forward.*)

FRAN. Everything was different in the sixties.

BRIAN. Hitchhiking around the courntry.

FRAN. Sure. Denver.

BRIAN. Big Sur.

FRAN. Remember the sit-ins.

BRIAN. Yeah. Psychedelics.

FRAN. God. Timothy Leary.

BRIAN. Kerouac.

FRAN. R. Crumb comics.

BRIAN. Musk oil.

FRAN. *Siddhartha.*

BRIAN. Make love, not war.

FRAN. Yeah, but even sex was different then. It was like for the first time some of the bullshit barriers between men and women were coming down. Now I think a lot of people are back in the same old shit.

BRIAN. Like how?

FRAN. Well, like singles bars.

BRIAN. Yeah . . . Well, some of them are OK.

FRAN. Oh, yeah, well *some* are. I just go there for a drink anyway.

BRIAN. Oh, me too. (*Pause.*)

FRAN. I'd forgotten about musk oil.

BRIAN. Yeah, Pachouli.

FRAN. Pachouli.

BRIAN. It was supposed to make you smell natural.

FRAN. It didn't make you smell natural. It made you smell like a weasel.

BRIAN. One thing though.

FRAN. What's that?

BRIAN. If I'd known what marijuana would eventually sell

for in the eighties, there's one thing I'd have done in the sixties.

FRAN. What would you have done?

BRIAN. Stockpiled. (*Mike, Kevin and Sally come forward.*)

MIKE. It's never gonna be the same.

SALLY. I know I'm never gonna get over this.

MIKE. I feel like I'm dead. (*Pause.*) Who's got a joint?

SALLY. I do. (*They light up and pass the joint.*)

KEVIN. It's good to be with family at a time like this. I mean, y'know, people who understood John. We're all family.

SALLY. All mankind's a family, Kevin.

KEVIN. I know that.

SALLY. I mean, that's what he was trying to say.

KEVIN. Don't you think I know that.

SALLY. Give peace a chance, Kevin, that's all.

KEVIN. I'd give peace a chance! Hey, you're not the only one who understood what he was saying.

SALLY. You never listened to the lyrics, Kevin.

KEVIN. I did too.

SALLY. Imagine all the people, Kevin.

KEVIN. I can imagine them.

SALLY. I don't think you can, Kevin, I think you're too self-centered Kevin, to imagine all the people.

KEVIN. Well, I can't imagine *all* the people. There are too many people to imagine *all* the people. I mean there are nine million people in New York. You want me to imagine them *all*. Get serious.

SALLY. Boy—did *you* miss the point.

MIKE. Oh wow! Oh wowwww!

SALLY. What?

KEVIN. What is it?

MIKE. Oh wow! I just had this flash! You know you were talking about all the people, and I thought about over-population and overcrowding, and then I realized this *is* a crowd. I mean we're in a crowd.

KEVIN. So?

25

MIKE. It's like that sermon Father McCaffrey gave last week about the time of the end.

KEVIN. I don't remember it.

SALLY. Naturally, Kevin, you were asleep.

MIKE. (*Rapidly.*) Remember, it was all about Christ having to be born in the stable because there was no room in the inn because everything was overcrowded and there was no room. And how that these were the final days because the time of the end is a time where you're going to have massed armies, and wars, and huge *crowds* and men "withering away for fear" and how the time of the end was the time of the *crowd*. And that's why Christ had to be born separate because he couldn't be born in the crowd. There was no *room* for him in the crowd. And we're *in* a crowd, and we have wars, and missiles, and bombs, and there's no place you can go to get away from it, because it's like there's no room because the time of the end is the time of no room. (*Pause.*)

SALLY. Oh wowwwww.

KEVIN. He's been like this all day. (*Brian and Fran come forward again.*)

FRAN. I had a brother . . .

BRIAN. . . . Had?

FRAN. He's dead now.

BRIAN. I'm sorry, how?

FRAN. He was killed in Viet Nam.

BRIAN. Oh, I'm sorry.

FRAN. Killed in a goddamn senseless war. Don't get me wrong. He was a patriot. He won medals. I guess he killed people. I know he killed people. But he was always a sensitive kid y'know. Real quiet. He listened to the Beatles and Jimmy Hendrix y'know. It wasn't like he was right wing or anything but he was drafted. His number came up and he had to go to that goddamn senseless war. Jesus. He wouldn't have understood America now. He wouldn't have understood what he died for. I know he wouldn't. I mean Watergate — Yassir Arafat, then Khomeni, this. This world isn't what he died for. Kenny wouldn't have understood a world like this.

(*Pause.*) Did you go to Viet Nam?

BRIAN. No. I, uh, have flat feet.

FRAN. I see. That's very fortunate.

BRIAN. I know.

FRAN. Goddamn senseless war. (*Silvio and Gately step forward. Rather secretively Silvio discreetly counting a wad of bills.*)

SILVIO. Sixty . . . Sixty-five, six and seven. Aw right. (*He offers Gately his share. Gately considers it. Shakes his head "no."*) What's the matter with you?

GATELY. Nothing. I just don't want it, that's all.

SILVIO. Jesus Christ. You're gonna act like this even after I told you about Cambodia? You're livin' in a corrupt country, my friend. It's a jungle. Just like in 'Nam. You do it to the other guy before he does it to you. You know who said that ?

GATELY. Who?

SILVIO. Marlon Brando in "On the Waterfront." And it's just as true now as it was then. The whole system is geared like that. They wanna keep all the have nots fightin' each other. They don't want anybody to heal or get better. They want the drunks to stay drunks, the whores to stay whores, the junkies to stay junkies, the blacks to stay in the ghetto, and us to stay crooks.

GATELY. I'm . . . not a crook.

SILVIO. Oh really. What are you then, a brain surgeon?

GATELY. I'm not a crook . . . I served my country. I did it. (*Pause.*) I did it.

SILVIO. I did it too. Big fuckin' deal. (*Silvio and Gately stare at each other.*) Take it. (*Gately looks at his share. Slowly he reaches out and takes it.*) That's better. (*The volume comes up on Larry's radio. Playing "Revolution."* Morris is obviously upset. Larry sneers at him. Morris winces, peers closer at radio. Squints closely at the different knobs. Irritated, Larry looks the other way. With unexpected swiftness, Morris reaches out, switches the radio off. Puts his hand in his*

---

*See Special Note on copyright page.

pocket and looks the other way. Larry is stunned. He reaches
down to turn on the radio.)
LARRY. Hey fossil-face! What you done?
MORRIS. (*Innocently.*) Are you addressing me?
LARRY. Damn right! Where's my knob?
MORRIS. Knob? What knob?
LARRY. I'll be damned! Man stole my knob and he won't even admit it. Gimme my knob before I bust your nose for you.
MORRIS. I don't know what you're talking about.
LARRY. I'm talking bout my knob for my cassette. The one you stole.
MORRIS. I know nothing about a knob.
LARRY. Fork over that knob, honky, or I'm gonna roust you out for damn sure.
MORRIS. You lay one finger on me and I'll yell bloody murder. I'll tell them you attacked me. They'll throw you in Sing Sing. (*Pause.*)
LARRY. I can't believe this shit. I gotta goddamn senile honky on my hands. (*Pause.*) Gimme my knob. (*Larry begins to go for Morris.*)
MORRIS. (*Hissing.*) Watch it! Watch it! This place is crawling with cops. You make one false move and they'll be down your throat like a pack of dogs! (*Larry looks around. There are dozens of cops.*)
LARRY. Man, you're the one that's got the knob. You're the one they'll arrest.
MORRIS. They won't arrest me.
LARRY. Why not?
MORRIS. Because I'm a little old man. (*Morris smiles. They recede. Fran and Brian step forward.*)
FRAN. Love is the greatest energy in the world.
BRIAN. I know.
FRAN. Yeah, but did you know they proved that?
BRIAN. Did they prove that?
FRAN. Absolutely. It has an energy, an aura. It's a source of life. It has an electric field.

28

BRIAN. Wait. I think I've heard that when people make love they give off an electrical, uh, whatever, impulses.

FRAN. Right. We get it from each others skin.

BRIAN. (*Slight beat.*) You've got nice skin.

FRAN. (*Slight beat.*) Thank you. I take care of my skin. It's one of my best features. Thank you.

BRIAN. Well, you do. (*Pause.*) What's your name again?

FRAN. Fran.

BRIAN. That's right. (*Pause.*) So. Do you like art, Fran?

FRAN. I love art.

BRIAN. So do I. I spend all my time in galleries.

FRAN. Do you really?

BRIAN. Oh sure.

FRAN. Have you seen the Hopper exhibit at the Whitney?

BRIAN. No.

FRAN. You must see that.

BRIAN. Oh, I'm definitely going to see that. (*Pause.*)

FRAN. I didn't realize he lived so long.

BRIAN. Who?

FRAN. Hopper.

BRIAN. Did he?

FRAN. Yeah. He died in '67.

BRIAN. '67? Well . . . at least he lived long enough to hear the Beatles.

FRAN. Yeah.

BRIAN. But not long enough to hear Abbey Road. (*Pause. They stare forward blankly.*)

FRAN. There's a very melancholy strain in the work of Edward Hopper. A lack of detail in the faces. He captures the mundane quality of existence. And that desperate quality within that mundaneness. I mean, his people look at each other but they don't see each other. Most of the times they don't even look at each other. They don't reach out and touch each other. They just wait. With that awful blankness. In nighthawk dinners, in quiet Sunday roadside windows, forgotten gas station, over chop suey they wait. There's this one where there are no people, just the trees and the grass, and it seems to rustle as if a disturbing wind were passing by. And there's a great sense of urgency and expectancy in the woods. Something is about to happen. The woods are waiting, waiting. Waiting. Just waiting for the answer. But waiting quietly and darkly in a woodsy sort of way. There's this other one where a group of people are waiting in like reclining deck chairs like at a resort only they're facing mountains, like Arizona mountains, with a vast desert that sweeps before them and they're all dressed up as if they were waiting to be beckoned, to be called, to be taken across this vast lunar landscape By who? By what? By death? By God? By flying saucers? What power will take them? What power are they waiting for? I don't know. Who knows? (*With significance.*) But this much I do know. They're very placid as they wait. They are not disturbed, show no anxiety, they are placid. (*Pause.*) And here we are. A group of strangers looking at this building where he lived. Waiting for an answer. Waiting for understanding. Waiting for forgiveness? Waiting for something. That's for damn sure. (*Silvio and Gately move forward.*)

SILVIO. Aw yeah. When you're a kid, you can afford to believe in all that Santa Claus bullshit. People helping each other. But out on the streets it's different. I saw buddies of mine blown away so many times, it got to where, I didn't wanna make anymore friends. I mean, to the people pushin' the buttons, I was just a statistic. Well, I'm through bein' a statistic. From now on, I'm gonna be a human being. (*Pause. They recede. Larry and Morris move forward.*)

LARRY. Gimme that goddamn knob before I turn you into a statistic.

MORRIS. Violence will get you nowhere in life.

LARRY. I'll call the cops.

MORRIS. You won't do a thing. You're afraid of the police.

LARRY. I ain't scared a no cops.

MORRIS. You've probably got a record.

LARRY. I ain't got no record.

MORRIS. I'll bet you do. I'll bet you've got a record.

LARRY. I ain't got no record.

MORRIS. You're being defensive.

LARRY. I ain't got much of a record

MORRIS. I knew it!

LARRY. Gimme the knob.

MORRIS. I knew it! This town is crawling with thieves, crime, and corruption, mugging, killings, rapings! It's like a sewer.

LARRY. Then why don't you move?

MORRIS. What?! And leave New York?

LARRY. Gimme the knob.

MORRIS. On one condition.

LARRY. Whatever.

MORRIS. First you gotta hear the condition.

LARRY. Ok. What is it?

MORRIS. You agree?

LARRY. Yeah, yeah!

MORRIS. Talk to me.

LARRY. . . . Huh?

MORRIS. Talk to me.

LARRY. What else?

MORRIS. Nothing else. Just talk to me.

LARRY. Why?

MORRIS. Because. I don't have anyone to talk to.

LARRY. Yeah, and I know why.

MORRIS. Why?

LARRY. Because nobody likes you.

MORRIS. People like me!

LARRY. Nobody likes you. You're the meanest man in the whole building.

MORRIS. No I'm not! No I'm not! That's a twenty-story building!

LARRY. Big deal. You're still the meanest.

MORRIS. Mrs. Kravowitz.

LARRY. She's not mean. She's crazy.

MORRIS. Still, no one talks to her.

LARRY. She's crazy.

MORRIS. I used to talk to her.

LARRY. Yeah! Did she make any sense?

MORRIS. Nah. She's crazy. You say, "Hello, Mrs. Kravo-witz." She starts yelling, screaming, banging doors. You know what she's afraid of?

LARRY. What?

MORRIS. Cossacks.

LARRY. Cossacks.

MORRIS. Cossacks.

LARRY. How can you figure that?

MORRIS. You don't have to figure that. The woman's crazy. Gone. Bonkers. Screaming and yelling like that. Mr. Kravowitz did the right thing.

LARRY. What do you mean? He died last month.

MORRIS. That's what I mean. He did the right thing. He checked out early. Who could live with a woman like that? Crazy . . . Mr. Bennario?

LARRY. What about him?

MORRIS. No one talks to him.

LARRY. Of course not. He's deaf in both ears and he's had a stroke.

MORRIS. I know. He's a complete waste of time. I used to say hello to Mr. Bennario.

LARRY. What'd he say?

MORRIS. Nothin'. He's deaf in both ears and he's had a stroke. The man's pathetic. Like talking to a wall. But lemme tell you something. Even when he could hear, and he could talk back he didn't have a lot to say. The stroke just completed the job. Yes sir, all that man can do now is drool. Have you ever noticed that? That man can really drool. Drools constantly. Mouth like a faucet. If they ever make an Olympic event outta drooling the man could be another Jim Thorpe. His sweater's always wet. It's disgusting. I don't like to get on the elevator with him. I wait for the next car. I say, "Goodbye, Mr. Bennario!" he doesn't hear me . . . the man's stone deaf. Depressing individual. I don't like to be around him.

LARRY. That's what I don't like about that building. Too many old people!

MORRIS. Hey, listen! Old people are invaluable! We are the link with the enormous past!

LARRY. Yeah? Well, I live in the enormous present.

MORRIS. Horse feathers. The present is vastly overrated. You think this is important? Look you say, "Right NOW, this is the present!!" "Triumph!" Big deal. It's already the past. I know the past. I've been there . . . I knew Babe Ruth.

LARRY. You knew Babe Ruth?

MORRIS. Sure, he was a pussycat. Lived around the corner. What an appetite! Say! You wanna know about history I'm your man!

LARRY. I don't want to hear about history man! They got history rigged. They say there weren't no black cowboys in the old West. Now, that's gotta be some sorta lie cause everything you read tells you there were thousands a brothers out there in the west along with John Wayne and the rest of 'em. But they got it all rigged.

MORRIS. Who is "They"?

LARRY. "They" is "Them" man.

MORRIS. Who is "Them"?

LARRY. "They" is Them that keeps you down. They is now cause you are then. They is right cause you is wrong. They is hard cause you is soft. They is up cause you is down. They is who they are cause you is who you *are not*. They up while you down. They is cause you ain't. They smile cause you frown. They gots cause you wants. They night is your day. Their birth is your death. Their smile is your tear. (*He stops with the routine.*) . . . Got it.

MORRIS. (*Impressed.*) You should have been a poet.

LARRY. What the hell you think I am? (*Kevin, Mike, Sally.*)

KEVIN. We're gonna stay here all day.

SALLY. I gotta be home by 5:30.

KEVIN. What do you mean?

SALLY. My mother wants me home.

33

KEVIN. When are you going to stop listening to your mother?

SALLY. You've never liked my mother.

KEVIN. What's to like? She's like an ogre; she's domineering, she's bossy, she's a pain in the ass.

SALLY. And your mother isn't?

KEVIN. Hey, watch what you say about my mother.

SALLY. Boy! Boys and their mothers.

KEVIN. What about it?

SALLY. It's a proven complex. You love your mother. Come on, admit it!

KEVIN. I love my mother.

SALLY. (*Turning to Mikey.*) What about you?

MIKE. I love my mother, too.

SALLY. Men are so gross.

FRAN. Women basically love men.

SILVIO. Man is the warrior.

MORRIS. What're you gonna do for a career?

LARRY. I got a career.

MORRIS. What's that?

LARRY. I'm going to be a comic.

MORRIS. A comic?

LARRY. Yeah. Anything wrong with that?

MORRIS. Well, so far you're not funny.

LARRY. I'm not tryin' to be funny.

MORRIS. Good. Cause so far you're not.

LARRY. I'm not tryin'.

MORRIS. Cause the bottom line is you gotta be funny.

LARRY. I'm funny. Ok. I'm funny. People die laughin'. They die! One of these days you're gonna see a headline in the newspaper—"Comic Too Funny; 500 Die Laughing"

MORRIS. Where do you do this comedy?

LARRY. (*Irate.*) Where do you think? Where do you think? Just where the hell do you think?

MORRIS. Inna night club.

LARRY. . . . No, in a pool hall. Well. Once in a club.

MORRIS. How did it go?

LARRY. I was a little nervous, huh? I was just a little nervous.

MORRIS. You flopped.

LARRY. Yeah, but I'm better in a pool hall.

MORRIS. Yeah, sure, I know how it is.

LARRY. How do you know?

MORRIS. I used to be in vaudeville.

LARRY. . . . You in vaudeville.

MORRIS. Yeah, sure. Did an act with a seal. Played the harmonica.

LARRY. You played the harmonica?

MORRIS. No, the seal played the harmonica.

LARRY. Nooo—

MORRIS. Yeah, sure. Right before vaudeville died.

LARRY. Yeah and now I know what killed it.

MORRIS. That's very funny. Well, lemme see some.

LARRY. See some what.

MORRIS. Comedy.

LARRY. Oh man, you wouldn't get it.

MORRIS. I'm a very good audience.

LARRY. You're senile.

MORRIS. I'm sharp as a tack. What's the matter, you scared.

LARRY. Scared.

MORRIS. You're petrified.

LARRY. Ok! Ok! Here I'll give you some. "Ladies and gentlemen, I was in this bar the other night. And this big motherfucker comes in . . . "

MORRIS. Hey! Hey!

LARRY. What?

MORRIS. That word!

LARRY. What word!

MORRIS. The "M" word!

LARRY. Motherfuck—

MORRIS. Don't say it again.

LARRY. Why not?

MORRIS. You shouldn't say those words in public.

LARRY. It is social satire.

MORRIS. It is nasty.

LARRY. They're just words.

MORRIS. You say those words in front of your mother?

LARRY. Well . . . no.

MORRIS. Why not?

LARRY. My father he be whippin' my ass.

MORRIS. See there! Anything you can't say in front of your mother you shouldn't say in public. Bodily functions are not funny.

LARRY. Just cause it ain't funny to you don't mean it ain't funny.

MORRIS. The world's going to the shit heap.

LARRY. Just cause you're going to the shit heap don't mean the world's going to the shit heap.

MORRIS. I'm not going to the shit heap! I gotta stomach made of cast iron. Here! Punch me inna stomach.

LARRY. Get outta here—

MORRIS. C'mon.

LARRY. No.

MORRIS. Why not?

LARRY. I don't want to.

MORRIS. C'mon. You chicken?

LARRY. No.

MORRIS. Then c'mon!

Larry. No.

MORRIS. Like cast iron.

LARRY. No.

MORRIS. You're chicken. Like cast iron! (*Larry gives him the merest tap. Morris gasps. Doubles over. Fran runs over to help. Morris brushes her away. Gasping.*) That's the trouble with the world today—no respect for the elderly. (*Kevin, Sally, Mikey.*)

KEVIN. That's the trouble with the whole thing. Older people don't have respect for *us* as people. They don't have any respect for our lifestyle.

SALLY. Kevin, we're in high school. We don't have a life style.

KEVIN. That's not true. We have a life style.

SALLY. What is it? Smoking dope. Is that your life style, Kevin?

KEVIN. No! My life style is like, expanding myself on a spiritual plane of being.

SALLY. How do you do that Kevin? By going to Central

36

Park and doing drugs?

KEVIN. Look, John was a very spiritual person. That's why all these people are here. He was the soul of an age. Not like say . . . Elvis.

SALLY. Yeah, there wasn't this big of a turnout for Elvis.

KEVIN. Of course not. Elvis was just this fat disgusting old man that played Vegas.

SALLY. My parents have all his records . . . but they never play them anymore.

MIKE. Elvis was interesting though in an historical sort of way. I mean, he had a lot of punk in him.

KEVIN. Yeah, but the Beatles took rock and roll and turned it into a major religious force? I mean, they really popularized Eastern religion.

SALLY. But Kevin, you don't even believe in Eastern religion.

KEVIN. Bullshit? I just can't practice Eastern religion at home.

SALLY. What?

KEVIN. Get serious. You think my mother's gonna cook a macro-biotic diet?

MIKE. But you meditate don't you Kevin?

KEVIN. Huh? That's right, I meditate!

SALLY. Ha! I don't believe you meditate Kevin. I think it's some sort of scam.

KEVIN. Well, I do! I meditate!

SALLY. Ha! You fall asleep watching T.V. How can you meditate?

KEVIN. Well, why don't you shut your mouth Sally cause I meditate!

SALLY. You don't meditate!

KEVIN. Well, you don't masturbate!

SALLY. I what?! I don't what?

KEVIN. You heard me.

SALLY. I can't believe you said that!

MIKE. I didn't hear anything.

SALLY. You said you'd never tell anybody that!

MIKE. He really didn't say that.

SALLY. He said it all right.

KEVIN. Look I'm sorry. I was pissed because you said I didn't meditate.

SALLY. Who do you meditate with Kevin? Rhoda Fahrquhar?

KEVIN. He we go. Rhoda Fahrquhar.

MIKE. Look, you two shouldn't break up over Rhoda Fahrquhar. She's just a stupid person!

SALLY. (*Crying.*) With big tits!

KEVIN. Sally! I'm sorry.

SALLY. Just cause she'll do it with anybody!

KEVIN. Sally—

SALLY. Does she masturbate, Kevin? I'll bet she masturbates, Kevin! You meditate and she masturbates! I hope you're very happy together!

KEVIN. You've got it wrong—

SALLY. Oh? You masturbate and she meditates? Great. Masturbation. At least we're finally talking about something. A subject of which you have first-hand knowledge. And I do mean hand.

KEVIN. Sally—

SALLY. I hope it drops off, Kevin. (*She begins crying.*)

MIKE. Would you guys quit it? We're here for John remember? . . . Besides you guys have someone to love. You're the lucky ones. I've never been in love. Love is something I just don't understand. (*Silvio and Gately step forward.*)

SILVIO. You take men and women.

GATELY. OK.

SILVIO. A guy meets a chick and right away what's he thinkin?

GATELY. Whether she's a nice girl.

SILVIO. Get outta here. What're you kiddin'. He's thinkin' how can I knock myself off a little piece of this. He's thinkin' tits and ass and legs and thighs and navels.

GATELY. Navels.

SILVIO. Yeah, navels.

GATELY. What? She got more than one?

SILVIO. Gately.

GATELY. You said navels. Na-*vels*. What is this girl, some kinda freak?

SILVIO. Listen to me.

GATELY. Where does she keep this other navel? In her purse? (*Silvio slaps him on the arm.*)

SILVIO. Would you listen to what I'm saying and learn?

GATELY. OK.

SILVIO. OK?

GATELY. OK.

SILVIO. So. OK, men and women.

GATELY. OK.

SILVIO. Basically, Gately, it's like this. Men have to perform for women in order to repopulate the species. Women are *subconsciously* attracted to men who will make a good mate.

GATELY. What about your sister?

SILVIO. Well, *my* sister married an asshole. My point is: Men have to prove themselves to prove that they're a good mate. And you do that by having status. And you have the status by being the meanest mother fucker in the valley. Man is the aggressor, man is the warrior. This is confirmed through thousands of years of genetics. In order to get—say that woman over there—which isn't a bad idea, considering (*Gesture.*)—in order to get that, I gotta come through. I gotta be a provider. I gotta have money to buy her things.

GATELY. Like what?

SILVIO. Classy chick like that—probably a sports car.

GATELY. A sports car.

SILVIO. Probably.

GATELY. Just to get laid! It's not worth it.

SILVIO. All I'm sayin' is she's classy.

GATELY. Still—a sports car.

SILVIO. All I'm sayin' is you gotta make it worth their while. These classy east side type women—they look at me or any guy like me—and you know what they're thinking.

GATELY. That you're crude.

SILVIO. That is not what they're thinkin'.

GATELY. You're a thief.

SILVIO. I'm a professional. Observe that distinction.

GATELY. OK. You're a professional thief.

SILVIO. Thank you. And I'm not crude, you asshole.

GATELY. You're not.

SILVIO. No, I'm not. You know what I am?

GATELY. What?

SILVIO. You know what I got? Animal magnetism.

GATELY. Wah.

SILVIO. Yeah.

GATELY. Really?

SILVIO. It's true.

GATELY. How ya know?

SILVIO. A girl in Jersey told me. When women see me they melt down like Three Mile Island.

GATELY. No kiddin'?

SILVIO. Basically, I could have any woman in the world.

GATELY. Raquel Welch?

SILVIO. Sure.

GATELY. Naw, you don't even know her phone number.

SILVIO. Look. This is only a theory.

GATELY. I know it is.

SILVIO. My point is: I could maybe attract a woman—Raquel Welch, Bo Derek—I could get 'em maybe to go to bed, get 'em in the sack, give 'em the old pumperooni. But I could not—and this is the key thing about the whole thing—I could *not* get them to marry me until I got one thing.

GATELY. Yeah. A job.

SILVIO. Right! I'd have to get lots of money. That's the key thing you gotta have—money. If you want women—I mean classy women—you gotta have money.

GATELY. (*Pause.*) Is that what we're doin' all this for? (*Fran and Brian.*)

FRAN. I think a man is never sexier than when he's nurturing.

40

BRIAN. . . . Nurturing what?

FRAN. Nurturing within a relationship.

BRIAN. I see.

FRAN. Men can be very nurturing.

BRIAN. Oh, I know they can. I'm very nurturing myself.

FRAN. Are you?

BRIAN. Yeah. Sure. (*Pause.*)

FRAN. I think it was beautiful what Lennon was getting into.

BRIAN. Yeah, me too.

FRAN. How do you know?

BRIAN. What?

FRAN. That you agree with me.

BRIAN. When?

FRAN. Just now. You agreed with me before you knew what I was going to say.

BRIAN. I sensed that I would agree with you.

FRAN. Huh.

BRIAN. I think our personalities are very agreeable.

FRAN. Oh. (*Silvio and Gately.*)

SILVIO. A man will agree to anything in order to get laid. He'll agree to go to a movie he's already seen, he'll agree that black is white and white is black. Day is night, night is day. If she says jump, he'll say "how high." A man will agree to anything, no matter how stupid, in order to get laid. (*Pause. Fran and Brian.*)

FRAN. The thing I was going to say is that I think it was beautiful when Lennon started doing that whole househusband number.

BRIAN. Huh.

FRAN. Househusband—you know, where he stayed home and baked the bread and took care of the kid and she went off and talked to the lawyers. I think that's terrific.

BRIAN. Oh I agree. Terrific. (*Pause.*) Say, are you a feminist?

FRAN. It's inconceivable to me that a woman living in the world today could not be a feminist.

BRIAN. Oh I agree. If I were a woman, I'd be a feminist.

FRAN. You can be a feminist and be a man. The two ideas are not mutually exclusive.

BRIAN. Oh I agree. I consider myself a feminist. I was one of the first guys to read "The Naked Eunuch."

FRAN. You mean "The Female Eunuch."

BRIAN. Yeah. That's the one. (*Pause.*) So . . . you're a secretary, huh?

FRAN. Yeah, we've established that. You're in what? Advertising.

BRIAN. That's right! Advertising. Y & R. Uh. Y & R. Young and Rubicam?

FRAN. OK. ·

BRIAN. Ever heard of them?

FRAN. No.

BRIAN. Well, we're one of the biggest. One of the giants. We're really, really big. Really big.

FRAN. Do you like working for a big company?

BRIAN. Fran, not especially. But enough about me Fran, let's talk about you. So you live on the East Side.

FRAN. That's right.

BRIAN. That's so interesting. I live in the East 80's.

FRAN. I live in the East 70's.

BRIAN. What an incredible coincidence. You know, I was at a bar when it happened. When this happened. All this. We couldn't believe it. None of us. It was horrible. Y'know. The sheer disbelief. In fact, if I had to characterize modern life and times in one phrase, I would have to say it's a feeling of disbelief. Because I was there and someone said "John Lennon has been shot." And there was a silence—a silence of disbelief—then someone said—"yeah John's dead and Paul is the walrus." . . . And a few people laughed. Then it sunk in. Then people started drinking again and getting picked up. Business as usual. (*Pause.*) I've never seen *The Unicorn* that depressed. Say, the Unicorn's in the East 70's . . . Do you know it?

FRAN. Yes.

BRIAN. Do you ever go there?

FRAN. No.

BRIAN. Oh.

FRAN. (*Pause.*) I sometimes stop off at Ladyfingers for a drink.

BRIAN. Oh sure! I know Ladyfingers! I go there sometimes.

FRAN. (*Defensively.*) I just stop off there sometimes for a quick drink. After work, I mean. It relaxes me.

BRIAN. Nothing like a quick drink after work.

FRAN. I rarely have more than one or two. I'm not a heavy drinker.

BRIAN. I know what you mean. I'm not a heavy drinker either, except when I am.

FRAN. But . . . It's a relief to have a drink after work. To unwind. To forget about work.

BRIAN. Hey—"When you work all day, you live for the nights."

FRAN. God, ain't it the truth!

BRIAN. That was one of ours.

FRAN. One of your what?

BRIAN. "When you work all day, you live for the nights." That was one of our slogans. For a client.

FRAN. What product?

BRIAN. I'm trying to think. It was either clothes or cosmetics. (*Pause.*) I'm very good at slogans. (*Larry and Morris.*)

MORRIS. You know what your problem is?

LARRY. Yeah—you.

MORRIS. Wait! Where are you going!

LARRY. Anywhere. I don't know.

MORRIS. I got the knob, remember.

LARRY. I'll get another one.

MORRIS. You can't just get an individual knob.

LARRY. You get the individual knob when you steal the individual radio.

MORRIS. You steal this radio? That's terrible. You should be out getting a job.

LARRY. Hey, man. There ain't no jobs for people like me.

43

The poor stay poor.

MORRIS. You think I came to this country rich or something.

LARRY. Well, at least when you got off the boat it wasn't in chains.

MORRIS. Listen to me—you steal—they throw you in prison.

LARRY. Man, I got news for you—this is a prison. All America is a prison. Have you ever read Ralph Ellison's *The Invisible Man*?

MORRIS. No, but I saw the movie with Claude Rains.

LARRY. Nooo—

MORRIS. I love the part where he's running through the snow and leaves the little footprints.

LARRY. No, man, it's a book about a black man in America that no one sees him for who he really is. Well, that's me. The invisible man. No one wants to see me for who I really am. My father, my mother, my teachers. No one wants to see me. They all want me to be someone else. So in my act I do other people. I do a white guy meeting a brother—"Hi there, brother, I call you brother, but I sure as hell don't want you marrying my sister. Ha-ha-ha!

MORRIS. Now, that's funny!

LARRY. I do God tap-dancing.

MORRIS. You do God tap-dancing? (*Pause.*) God's not doing anything.

LARRY. Sometimes God doesn't feel like tap-dancing.

MORRIS. Now that's funny!

LARRY. I do an old Jewish guy at Zabars. "Take a number? Vat do you mean take a number? I took a number. I lost my number. Wat do you mean take another number. I'm in line here."

MORRIS. Now that's not funny. Once I lost *my* number.

LARRY. Then they get the killer elbows going.

MORRIS. What killer elbows?

LARRY. Old people have killer elbows. It's like they sharpen 'em. And they be jabbin' you with them elbows. You're in

Macy's and they're elbowin' through the crowd—They get you right in the kidneys. Ppfft! Old people should have a sign on 'em! Warning: The surgeon general has determined that old people can be hazardous to your health.

MORRIS. That's definitely not funny.

LARRY. I do a junkie hanging out. "Hey, brother, spare a quarter, bro. Bro." (*The brother obviously has walked on by.*) "Lousy low-life mother-fucker! You ain't no brother of mine. Hell, I'd a been your father, that dog hadn't beat me up the stairs!"

MORRIS. Can I give you some free advice?

LARRY. Well, I sure as shit ain't gonna pay for it.

MORRIS. Be yourself.

LARRY. What?

MORRIS. Just be yourself—be yourself.

LARRY. . . . And just who do suppose that is. (*Larry begins to exit.*)

MORRIS. Wait! Wait! The knob; I've still got the knob. (*Larry returns.*)

LARRY. Here. Take the damn thing.

MORRIS. What're you doing? (*He slips the radio over Morris's head.*)

LARRY. My man, you are now the proud owner of a radio-cassette tape recorder. Wear it in good health.

MORRIS. No! Don't go! Don't steal anything. Please. Don't. Larry, listen.! Larry, Larry, don't go! Talk to me. (*Morris can't get the radio off his neck. One hand must support him with the cane. The other hand is too weak to get it off his neck. When he tries with one hand to get it off, he totters and near falls. He switches cane to other hand. This doesn't work either. He sighs. Turns on the radio: "Eleanor Rigby": —The refrain: "Ah look at all the lonely people."*)* (*Silvio and Gately.*)

SILVIO. Did you realize this whole city was built cause some guy wanted to get laid?

*See Special Note on copyright page.

GATELY. What?

SILVIO. All those skyscrapers down there are like guys pricks. It's the truth. And look at it. It's violent. It's dirty. It's falling apart. It's broke. People can never get a cop when they need one—which is a good thing for us—people don't understand how this city came into being. See, people came here to make money. To gain power. To get filthy rich. And what's a guy tryin' to make money for?

GATELY. To get laid?

SILVIO. Essentially. To get some chick, to get married. Even when those rich guys get married they got mistresses. They got 'em stashed all over town. They hide 'em like squirrels hide nuts.

GATELY. Where do they hide 'em?

SILVIO. Everywhere. They got 'em stashed all over. Like in East Side apartments you know real chic y'know. Fancy places y'know. Hi-Fi's. Pool tables. Disposals. The latest appliances. All sorts of great furniture y'know. Carpets as thick as steaks. Y'know they got terraces so they can sunbathe naked, who look down on other people who sunbathe naked. It's like the domino theory applied to filthy-rich naked people. They got it all. Naked women in fancy apartments. They're everywhere. East Side, West Side, Uptown, Downtown. Soho. Chelsea. Brooklyn. Queens. If you're not a rich executive, if you're just a poor executive, you got one maybe in, like, Union City. Some are so rich they got 'em on the West Coast and you know what all this is called?

GATELY. What.

SILVIO. Capitalism. It's using people like vacuum cleaners to clean up the mess you've made.

GATELY. Like objects.

SILVIO. Yeah, like things. Like the Army, you think the Army looks at you like a human being.

GATELY. No. Shit no.

SILVIO. The V.A.?

GATELY. Shit no!

SILVIO. Shit no is right. You're just a thing. Well, that's my whole point. As long as you're killin' things, it's ok. As long |

46

as they're not people. And it's ok. Like that woman over there. She looks at me. What does she see?

GATELY. Animal magnetism?

SILVIO. No. She sees a thing. She doesn't see me. Well that's what she is to me man, a thing. Just a thing. (*Pause.*) C'mon. (*They don't move. Brian and Fran.*)

FRAN. The thing is we really don't know each other.

BRIAN. I mean. What's to know, y'know, it's no big deal.

FRAN. No. It's like, people don't know each other, it's like we're all in our own compartment. Our own little box. (*They freeze. Morris begins to move slowly around the stage. Music: "Ticket to Ride."* He freezes. Mike, Kevin and Sally. Mike is still comforting Sally.*)

KEVIN. I can't believe you're making such a big deal.

SALLY. Women have emotions, Kevin, that's what you fail to understand.

KEVIN. What am I? Some insensitive piece of concrete?

MIKE. Kevin, you're making it worse.

SALLY. You sure picked a cruddy time to break up, Kevin. That's all I gotta say. It's really great that you picked this week to break up.

KEVIN. We didn't break up this week, Sally, we broke up three weeks ago.

SALLY. No! We said we were gonna *think* about breaking up three weeks ago. But did you think about it, Kevin? No you didn't think. You went out and dated Rhoda Fahrquhar. Probably screwed her! Probably got some sort of hideous v.d.! I hope you got the clap, Kevin. One of the most emotional weeks in the memory of man and you start taking out Rhoda Fahrquhar. Who you know I don't like anyway. You know something Kevin?

KEVIN. What?

SALLY. You *are* some insensitive piece of concrete.

KEVIN. Hey! I got feelings! I got feelings! I feel! You think I don't? Huh? Huh?

*See Special Note on copyright page.

47

SALLY. Are you crying, Kevin?

KEVIN. No.

SALLY. Are you trying to cry, Kevin?

KEVIN. Just leave me alone, o.k.? (*Fran and Brian.*)

FRAN. It's like spirals within spirals y'know. I mean I see images tumbling by. I see myself as a little girl on a visit to my grandmothers in Queens and we go to the park. And it's green and beautiful and my father's with me. Big, and young and strong. And whenever I think of that I think of "Penny Lane", it's like, that's the way it felt. (*Pause.*)

BRIAN. I know. It's like background music for our lives. I remember at my first high school dance and I was all sweaty and scared and I was gonna walk across the room to ask Richie Woodall to dance with me. And they started playing "Hey Jude" over the P.A. system. It was a Catholic dance. I think the nuns thought it was about St. Jude. The saint of lost causes.

FRAN. (*Passionately.*) Maybe that's what all this is. A lost cause. The sixties. The peace movement. Look what's happenin' now in the Middle East. El Salvador. Are we any closer? Are we getting there? Take a look at the E.R.A.? Are we getting there? Three-Mile Island. Are we getting there? How can we say we're civilized when we continue to hold people back. Because of sex, because of race. Is that getting us anywhere? Increased military spending, weapons for defense. (*Laughing.*) And the joke is we're all afraid of the bomb! We blame everything on "They." The Pentagon— "They"! The CIA—"They." But we all have to take responsibility for the society in which we live. All America wants to do is go to the movies! Is that getting us there? Where's the leadership? Where's the dialogue? We're not talking. We're not listening. We're missing the whole point. It's not the sixties. People are just burying their heads in the sand. People will do *anything* rather than be here now. (*Pause.*) Are we getting there? No. People are just going to the office and making money . . . People suck.

BRIAN. (*Impressed.*) Wow. You know, you're a very passionate woman.

FRAN. Well, what did you expect? Someone dumb?

BRIAN. No, it's just that women—

FRAN. Oh brother, here we go. It's just that women what?

BRIAN. Just that women that you meet in bars—

FRAN. Hey! You didn't meet *me* in a bar! Right? Get it?

BRIAN. But you said you *go* to bars.

FRAN. I go to bars. I wasn't born in a bar. Right?

BRIAN. It's just that I think you're very smart and very passionate and very attractive. And I don't meet women like that.

FRAN. Where do you meet your "women," Brian.

BRIAN. Bars. I meet my women in bars.

FRAN. Well, then maybe that's *your* problem. Brian. Maybe you're meeting those kind of women—the passionate, attractive, intelligent kind of women but since you're just living for the night, maybe you don't see them for what they are.

BRIAN. Hey. Who're you kidding? You go to bars. You have drinks. You meet guys.

FRAN. That's right, Brian. And I'm the passionate, attractive, intelligent kind. (*He touches her arm.*)

BRIAN. Look babe, I didn't mean to—

FRAN. Don't touch me.

BRIAN. O.k. I won't touch you.

FRAN. Boy I hate your kind.

BRIAN. My *kind*? My *kind*? Boy if that isn't sexual stereotyping I don't know what is.

FRAN. Granted. Sexual stereotyping. But in your case, it works.

BRIAN. Oh yeah? And what is my type?

FRAN. You're—the button-down-collar-junior-executive-climbing-the-ladder-of-success-but-I'm-really-the-sensitive-young-man type. That's your type. I'll bet you haven't been to a museum in a million years.

BRIAN. For your information just last week I went to the Museum of Modern Art.

FRAN. Oh yeah. What did you see?

BRIAN. Paintings.

49

FRAN. What kind of paintings?

BRIAN. Modern paintings

FRAN. Oh Jesus. What a fake. What a liar. I bet you weren't even at Woodstock.

BRIAN. I was too!

FRAN. Everybody has their little scheme don't they? Tell me, does this line work a lot? This I-like-art line? Does that work on everybody?

BRIAN. No. Just you.

FRAN. Well, it wasn't working on me. I can assure you of that.

BRIAN. Yeah, come to think of it, now, I've seen you before. Sure yeah. I see you all the time in the bars.

FRAN. You don't see me at bars.

BRIAN. Sure I do.

FRAN. You do not.

BRIAN. The Adams Apple, Michaels, Maxwells, The Meat Place, Martys, The Satyre, Pegasus, sure you're there all the time. You're not special. I thought you were but you're not. You're like all the rest.

FRAN. Fuck you.

BRIAN. My pleasure.

FRAN. One thing though.

BRIAN. Huh.

FRAN. If I'm like all the rest . . . so are you. (*Pause.*)

BRIAN. Look, I'm sorry . . . I don't know what we got so excited about . . . I mean . . . You're a nice girl.

FRAN. Woman.

BRIAN. Woman! Woman! Woman! (*Pause.*) Look . . . you wanna smoke . . . I've got some gum . . . spearmint . . . Look I'm not like this . . . maybe I am. I didn't used to be. I don't meet women like you. I felt alive in the sixties. That's why I came here. I wanted . . . I wanted . . . then I met you. I mean. Something. In common. I don't know. Maybe not. I didn't want to go to work. I wanted to talk. (*She accepts cigarette. He lights it.*) I mean. Life goes on. (*Silvio and Gately.*)

SILVIO. Everybody's got a scheme for takin' somebody else's money. The guy that sells cars. He's trying to take your money. The guy that sells life insurance, he's trying to take your money. The guy that's tryin' to make that girl, he's tryin' to take her money.

GATELY. Her money?

SILVIO. Sure. He wants to screw her but he doesn't want to pay for it. A whore or a wife, he'd have to pay for it. One way or another you gotta pay.

GATELY. But what about her. Doesn't she want to do it?

SILVIO. No. That's one of the great kept secrets of all time. Women don't like sex.

GATELY. What? Nahhhhh —

SILVIO. It's true.

GATELY. Look I knew a girl. She liked it and she liked it a lot.

SILVIO. Gately.

GATELY. She did. She'd do it anytime. Anytime her husband wasn't home.

SILVIO. Gately.

GATELY. Damn, be like getting caught in a mix-master.

SILVIO. Look. Women like sex.

GATELY. You just said they didn't.

SILVIO. Well, I'm talkin' the big picture.

GATELY. Well, let's talk the little picture. Where they still like it.

SILVIO. They like it. O.k.?

GATELY. Ya dang right they like it.

SILVIO. It's just that women are always looking for a mate. That's the important thing. They're scheming to get a mate. That's their way of takin' *your* money. That's their scheme. To get you to pay money into a marriage and a kid —

GATELY. A kid? I already got a kid?

SILVIO. Sure you got a kid.

GATELY. Shit.

SILVIO. Sure. And that's your money and her money all going into the kid. Life is a scheme. Everybody's got a scheme.

51

Women's scheme is to get a mate.

GATELY. I don't know if I buy all this. You know I slept with women all the time.

SILVIO. Yeah.

GATELY. And not one asked me to be their mate.

SILVIO. (*Pause.*) I can believe that.

GATELY. Not one.

SILVIO. Everybody's got a scheme. We spend our lives tryin' to figure out how to get the money. They scheme, I scheme. You scheme. (*Pause.*) In fact I wonder sometimes *what* you're schemin'. I mean what's goin' on in that brain of yours? I mean I know something's going on in there. (*Pause.*) It's kind a somethin' that irritates me. Your scheming. Like what are you thinkin' right now?

GATELY. I was thinking about the point man. We were on patrol moving into a village near An Loc. It had rained all morning. We were soaked through. And I thought of my father; that's right, I was thinking about my father and the Italian Campaign. My father was in the Italian Campaign. And I thought about my old man outside that village with wet feet. 'Cause I had wet feet too. And every step I took I felt like my father. I felt like I was stepping into my father's footsteps. It was fun. Pretending I was my father and I thought about Italy because . . . I don't know. It seems like a better place to have a war. At least you see familiar stuff. Like churches and stuff. Every now and then get some Italian food. And I was concentrating or pretending or whatever on the wet feet thing 'cause that's when they shot our ass off. I mean. They fuckin' blew our ass away. I mean we'd walked beyond where they were. I mean where they were. They were all around us. I mean the point man must have been fucking up or something, or not payin' attention or something 'cause he'd walked us right into 'em. And they got us all. They fuckin got everybody. Except the fuckin point man. They used to do that, y'know. Let the point man pass by. And then cut everybody else down. Get im all. Fuck it. But the point man must have been asleep or something or thinking about

52

his fuckin' wet feet. But he just laid there in the mud. He was wounded too but he knew that it wasn't bad and they never found him . . . They never found the point man. (*Pause.*) Let's do it.

SILVIO. Now you're talkin'. OK. Here's what happens with this one. I go over to those kids. The one in the parka I'll get him. You get the girl's purse. (*Silvio goes over to Sally, Mikey, Kevin.*) Say, you gotta light?

KEVIN. Uh, yeah. (*Silvio offers a cigarette to be lit. The kid lights it. All the while Gately behind them stands at a distance.*) Tough day, man. Tough day.

MIKE. It's really intense.

SILVIO. It's—yeah. That's a good word for it. I just had to be here y'know. I mean I came here. Had to be here for John!

MIKE. I know, I cut school. It's like they're a whole part of our lives.

SILVIO. Dig it. Y'know the Beatles meant a lot to me— 'cause I was in Nam, right?

KEVIN. You were in Nam?

SILVIO. Fuckin'A. (*To Sally.*) Pardon my French.

SALLY. That's OK. We cuss.

SILVIO. What's your name sweetheart?

SALLY. Sally.

SILVIO. Sally, Beautiful name. (*To Mike.*) Beautiful girl.

MIKE. She's not my girl. She's his girl.

SALLY. I am not. OK?

MIKE. Did you kill anybody?

SILVIO. When? (*Kevin starts giving Mike silent signals behind Silvio's back to quit talking to Silvio and for them to split.*)

MIKE. In Viet Nam.

SILVIO. (*Emotionally.*) Hey. Wow. Look. Y'know. That's a very—heavy thing, man. (*Silvio goes into his act. It looks like he is going to cry.*)

SALLY. Hey, Mikey. You shouldn't have asked that. It's like obviously a sensitive thing.

SILVIO. No, look, it's cool. Y'know if he doesn't ask how's

he gonna know. (*Pause.*) Yeah Mikey, I killed people.
MIKE. Oh God.
KEVIN. Why don't we get some coffee.
SILVIO. That's right, man. Oh God you get this feelin' right down to your socks this real, like you're gonna vomit feeling. But it's like, you gotta get over it man. It's kill or be killed. In the bush it's you or Charlie.
MIKE. Jesus. It's disgusting. How did you stand it?
SILVIO. It's something you get beyond. You gotta act like it ain't happenin'.
KEVIN. C'mon Mikey lets go get some coffee.
MIKE. No, this is interestin'. (*Kevin takes Sally's arm.*)
KEVIN. C'mon.
SALLY. No.
KEVIN. Coffee? Anyone for coffee?
MIKE. Look Kevin, don't order her around ok. You can't boss people, Kevin. You're not our father. (*Gately looking the other way, walks rapidly in the group, bumping into Kevin and Sally, Silvio, goes into the routine, causing a disturbance.*)
SILVIO. Hey, you! Watch where you're goin'.
GATELY. What's it to you?
SILVIO. What's it to me? You just bumped into my friends, that's what it is to me. (*During this Silvio begins bouncing Gately against Kevin and Sally giving Gately a chance to reach into Sally's purse to get the billfold.*) How ya like this guy, he comes over, bumps into people. Doesn't even apologize. Now I want you to apologize.
KEVIN. That's ok. No need.
GATELY. Who in the fuck asked you.
KEVIN. No, it's just that—(*Gately takes Kevin and shoves Kevin over to Silvio.*)
GATELY. You're lookin' for shit I can give it to you—
KEVIN. Next time I say lets get some coffee, can we just go get some coffee! (*They freeze. Brian and Fran.*)
FRAN. Look at that. Did you see that?
BRIAN. See what?

54

FRAN. That over there those two guys they just bumped into those kids.

BRIAN. So?

FRAN. There's something not right—I saw those two guys a
while ago. They were talking. They were friends. They were
hanging out—now they're fighting. That doesn't make any
sense. (*Pause.*) Did you see that?

BRIAN. I definitely didn't see that.

FRAN. That guy, the little one, he stuck his hand in the
girl's purse. He picked her purse. You saw it, you must have
seen it. We all saw it.

BRIAN. (*Evasively.*) I didn't see it. I didn't. (*Fran turning
around to the imaginary people in the crowd.*)

FRAN. Did anyone see that guy take that girl's purse? Did
anyone? C'mon you saw it. We all saw it. Jesus! Is this getting
us there? Is it getting us there? (*Morris begins to stagger
towards Fran, his voice choked by the radio strap. His voice
is a rasping cough. He raises his hand.*) There! You! I knew
someone saw.

MORRIS. Cchhffsst.

FRAN. You saw didn't you. C'mon. (*She takes him by the
arm and begins dragging him towards the "mugging" which
is still frozen. As the two groups get together the freeze
comes to life.*)

BRIAN. Where are you going?

FRAN. I'm going over there and help those kids; they're being shaken down by those two bums.

BRIAN. C'mon. You don't wanna . . .

FRAN. Get involved? Wanna bet. (*Fran goes over to the
group, dragging Morris along. She taps Silvio on the shoulder
as Silvio shoves Kevin away.*) Hey you.

SILVIO. Yeah, what's your problem, lady.

FRAN. I ain't got no problem. What's your problem.

SILVIO. Huh?

FRAN. What're you doin' with these kids?

SILVIO. Ain't doin' nothin' with 'em.

FRAN. Yeah, I saw him steal a girl's purse. (*To Morris.*) He saw it, too.

BRIAN. Fran . . .

SILVIO. She with you?

BRIAN. Uh, yeah.

FRAN. No.

BRIAN. No.

SILVIO. Get her outta here.

FRAN. (*To Sally.*) Check your purse.

SALLY. My purse.

SILVIO. Who *are* you? Policewoman?

FRAN. Check your purse. (*To Morris.*) He saw you, too.

SILVIO. (*To Morris.*) You saw me do what?

MORRIS. Cchhphggtt.

SILVIO. Look at him. He didn't see nothing. He's a old man. He's falling down and everything. (*Morris grabs Brian's arm gestures to the radio strap which is choking him.*)

BRIAN. What?

MORRIS. Ccchhffsst.

BRIAN. What's he saying?

MORRIS. (*Gasping.*) The strap . . . the strap . . .

MIKE. I think he's saying the strap.

BRIAN. Oh. (*Brian lifts the strap off Morris's neck. Morris takes a deep breath as he straightens up.*)

MORRIS. Aaaaaaahhh!

SALLY. Hey, my purse *is* gone.

BRIAN. I guess it was the strap. That thing's heavy. (*Brian releases the strap. It snaps back on Morris's neck. Morris gasps and is pulled lopsided again.*)

MIKE. (*To Brian.*) Hey I think he's chokin' again.

BRIAN. I think your right.

FRAN. Well, *do* something.

SALLY. Hey, my purse is gone.

FRAN. (*Brian lifts the strap.*) I can't believe you. You had to think about liftin' the strap. You see a man chokin' to death and you have to *think* about what to do? No! You don't have to think! You act! You do something! You offer aid.

56

MORRIS. Yeah. What she said.

SALLY. My purse really is gone.

KEVIN. I told you not to trust those guys.

FRAN. (*To Silvio.*) See there.

SILVIO. See there. See there what? Do you see a purse on me? I don't see no purse.

MIKE. (*To Kevin.*) What's the matter? These guys, they pickpockets.

SILVIO. Pickpockets?

GATELY. Pickpocket. I ain't no pickpocket.

MORRIS. (*To Brian.*) Would you take this off me? It's killing me.

BRIAN. (*Pulling the radio off.*) You know, you really ought to get something lighter. This is too heavy. (*Brian absently puts it over his shoulder. The dialogue that follows is a mishmash.*)

SALLY. So what about my purse?

KEVIN. Yeah.

GATELY. Purse? I ain't got no purse.

FRAN. Buncha' bums. You're young, you're strong . . .

MORRIS. When you've got your health you've got everything.

FRAN. You should be out working.

MORRIS. Worked everyday of my life.

SILVIO. Bums? Who you calling bums, lady?

FRAN. You're the only bums here.

SILVIO. I fuckin' fought for my fuckin' country, what the fuck have you ever done?

FRAN. Plenty, buster.

SILVIO. What'd you do? March in a fuckin' parade.

FRAN. Yes, I marched in a parade to stop the killing—

SILVIO. When did a parade ever stop anything?

FRAN. While women and children were being killed!

SILVIO. You don't have to tell me, lady, I was there!

FRAN. Killing women and children? What'd they do? Give you a medal for that?

SILVIO. As a matter of fact, I've got medals, yeah!

FRAN. That's something to be proud of.

SILVIO. Who says I'm proud of it?

FRAN. And I had a brother killed in Viet Nam.

SILVIO. Yeah, and if he were here today he'd be just like me.

MORRIS. I think I can clear this up, if everyone would just listen to me. You see, he's right and you're right—

SILVIO. Oh great! I got it now. I'm talking to one of those assholes who was out protesting the war while I was getting my ass shot off in Nam protecting you from democracy!

FRAN. You're damn right I was protesting! It was an immoral war, a racist war—

SILVIO. Look lady, you're not going to stop aggression—it's in the species.

FRAN. That's the kind of thinking that's going to start World War III! Well, "We won't die for your lies anymore!"

SILVIO. "WE"! What is this "we" shit? You weren't being drafted! You're blaming the war on the warriors! I walked with kings, lady!

FRAN. There's just no room for that kind of thinking anymore.

MIKE. Oh woow! No room! The time of the end is the time of no room!

KEVIN. Michael.

GATELY. What?

MIKE. The time of the end of all things is the time of the void. Of hopelessness. When there's no room for Jesus.

SILVIO. Hey kid. Let's leave Jesus out of this. OK?

GATELY. What's all this time of the end stuff?

KEVIN. Don't ask.

MIKE. It's like when God destroyed Sodom—He said "Get thee out of this city for I will destroy it." But they all thought he was joking.

GATELY. Who thought he was joking?

MIKE. Everyone!

GATELY. So what happened?

MIKE. He destroyed them.

GATELY. (*Angrily.*) Serves them right!

58

SALLY. Where's my purse?

MORRIS. What's your name?

BRIAN. Brian.

MORRIS. I was never sick a day in my life, Brian. Until last month, I had a gallstone operation.

FRAN. Just give her her purse.

SALLY. (*To Gately.*) I won't call the cops.

GATELY. You won't?

FRAN. Oh yes she will.

SILVIO. Oh yes she will.

FRAN. Aha! You admit it!

SILVIO. I ain't admittin' nothin. C'mon, get lost.

MORRIS. They found a couple of gallstones in me the size of golf balls. (*Larry wanders back on.*)

FRAN. You gonna give her the purse or not?

SILVIO. What purse, where?

FRAN. Am I gonna have to do something?

SILVIO. What're you gonna do.

LARRY. Hey man, that's my radio.

FRAN. Call a cop.

SILVIO. You're gonna call a cop.

FRAN. That's right. There's one right over there.

SILVIO. I wanna see you call the cop.

FRAN. Well, you're gonna see it.

LARRY. What're you doin' with my radio?

BRIAN. Huh.

LARRY. What is all this?

SILVIO. That's what I wanna know.

FRAN. I'm gonna count to ten.

SILVIO. Big deal. Count to ten. So what?

FRAN. One . . .

LARRY. Give the old man back his radio.

BRIAN. Huh.

LARRY. Is that all you got to say, Jack, is huh?

BRIAN. Huh.

FRAN. Two.

SILVIO. Two. Right.

LARRY. Gimme that radio before I beat the shit out of you.

BRIAN. Huh? Hey!

FRAN. Three.

MORRIS. It's all right.

LARRY. Nah it ain't. I gave it to you.

MORRIS. This is Brian. Brian, Larry.

BRIAN. How do you do.

FRAN. Four.

SILVIO. You can count to four. I'm impressed.

MORRIS. What's going on.

FRAN. Five.

KEVIN. Lady, it's only a purse.

SALLY. Yeah, but it's my purse, Kevin. You'd care if it was your purse.

FRAN. Six.

KEVIN. I'm a guy, I don't carry purses, Ok?

SALLY. Oh man, if it was just even a frisbie you'd practically fall down with a coronary.

LARRY. So he didn't steal it. Huh?

MORRIS. No, he's just holding it for me. It got a little heavy.

FRAN. You're not gonna get away with this.

SILVIO. Getta way with what. What is this "this"?

FRAN. The "this" is the victimization of the people. The people. The people of New York are fed up with . . .

BRIAN. This isn't yours? SILVIO. Oh, so now you're the voice of the people of New York.

MORRIS. It's a gift from my friend Larry, here. FRAN. Seven. You're gonna get it.

LARRY. Oh, man. SILVIO. I can't believe this. I just stopped to help these people out.

FRAN. Eight.

MORRIS. Why is she counting?

SILVIO. Is this a threat? Are you threatening me?

MORRIS. Y'know, this is really nice I haven't gotten

together with this many people in a long time.

FRAN. Nine.

MORRIS. Nine! Why am I counting?

SILVIO. You know what this is? A waste of time. I haven't got time for this.

MORRIS. What we ought to do is everyone exchange numbers so we can all get together again.

SILVIO. Why don't you do that, grandpa. Me? I'm leavin'. I can't do business this way. (*Silvio begins to walk off.*)

FRAN. You son-of-a-bitch, you're not going anywhere. (*Fran grabs him by the arm. Silvio flings it off viciously. Everyone tenses. Silence as everyone faces each other.*)

MORRIS. (*Quietly.*) Hey . . . hey, be nice. (*Gately takes the purse out of his jacket and hands it meekly to Sally.*)

FRAN. He didn't have the purse, huh?

SILVIO. I never said *he* didn't have it. (*Pause.*)

SALLY. Thank you.

GATELY. I'm . . . sorry.

KEVIN. What're you thankin' him for? He's a thief.

MORRIS. Funny, he looks like a nice boy . . . (*Gately blinking imcomprehensibly.*)

GATELY. I'm not a thief . . . I'm not . . . I'm a Vet . . .

MIKE. You're a veterinarian. (*Pause.*)

GATELY. (*Slowly.*) I'm a veteran. I was . . . in Viet Nam . . . I was there . . . where were you . . . (*He goes around the circle. For the first time it's obvious that he is mentally disturbed.*) Where were you . . . I was there . . . where were you . . . I was there . . . where were you . . . I was there . . . where were you . . . where were you . . . (*Pause.*)

MORRIS. I've lived in this neighborhood thirty-five years. (*Silvio goes to Gately. He puts his arm around Gately who seems to be drifting away. His words are slow and pained.*)

SILVIO. Hey. It's OK. Everything's OK. Calm down.

GATELY. Calm? How can I be calm? Did it happen or didn't it? Were we there or weren't we? Did this just happen or didn't it? We're not here. It all happened before. Tomorrow it'll all happen again. We'll be here in front of this place.

Or some place just like it. Or nearly. And people will be saying he's hysterical for telling the truth. The truth is we were here. We were witnesses. We forgot. We been here before but we just forgot. That's why it all seems so familiar. We've been here before. And things never change. They just get worse. And maybe whether we like it or not we should do something. Maybe we're the ones that're supposed to do it. So let's do it. We can't wait. Believe me. You can't trust the fuckin' assholes in the world. They'll blow it up everytime. So come on, don't wait for God—cause he ain't there—(*Screaming.*) Are you there? Are you there? Fuck you if you're there! You suck, you know that? You suck! (*Realizing the others are staring.*) You don't get it, do you? Silvio, even you don't get it. You're all asleep. You don't know what any of this means. FFFFUUUUCCCCKKKK. (*Quietly.*) Silvio . . . what's happenin' man?

SILVIO. Hey! C'mon! I'm here. Who cares what they think? They're just civilians. Just remember. You walked with kings.

GATELY. Yeah. (*Everyone watches them go. Sally snuggles up to Kevin who puts his arm around her. Brian and Fran exchange looks.*)

LARRY. (*Quietly.*) Yeah . . . he got it.

MIKE. Yeah. (*Slowly the different groups begin to split apart.*)

SALLY. What an awful day.

KEVIN. Yeah. C'mon let's get out of here. Let's walk down Broadway. (*They walk away from Mike. Sally stops. Mike has his back to them watching Silvio and Gately walk away.*)

MORRIS. I knew we should've exchanged numbers. (*Pause.*) You were ready to hit that guy cause he had my radio.

LARRY. Your radio? My radio!

MORRIS. My radio! You gave it to me.

LARRY. Ok, ok, ok. Your radio. (*Pause.*)

MORRIS. We had a good talk going there before you left. We gonna do it again sometime? (*No answer.*) I'll pay you. (*No answer.*) You like me!

LARRY. I keep tellin' you. You're the meanest man in the building.

MORRIS. I could talk to your father. I could tell him I'll pay you to talk to me.

LARRY. Don't do that.

MORRIS. Why not?

LARRY. He'll agree to it.

MORRIS. If you don't wanna do it — fuck it. (*Morris begins to exit.*)

LARRY. Hey — you just said the "F" word. (*Larry joins him.*)

MORRIS. What're you doing? You walking me home.

LARRY. Hey calm down Methuselah. I gotta see the old man anyway.

MORRIS. (*Gruffly.*) I'll show you my scrapbook from vaudeville. (*As they stroll off.*)

LARRY. You weren't kiddin' about that huh.

MORRIS. I did an act with a seal.

LARRY. Yeah, I know, you played the harmonica.

MORRIS. No, the seal played the harmonica. I played the ukelele.

LARRY. Now, this ain't no regular gig. (*They exit R. The other groups freeze. Brian and Fran. He lights her cigarette.*)

BRIAN. Wow! You were terrific.

FRAN. That felt good! That felt like the sixties.

BRIAN. Yeah . . . well.

FRAN. Well . . .

BRIAN. I gotta go to work.

FRAN. Me too.

BRIAN. So . . . goodbye.

FRAN. Goodbye. (*They shake. They part. They walk away. They turn. Brian goes to her. He goes to her urgently.*)

BRIAN. Fran!

FRAN. What!

BRIAN. Lemme buy you a drink.

FRAN. A drink?

BRIAN. C'mon.

FRAN. What about work?

BRIAN. To hell with it.

FRAN. Ok!

BRIAN. I'll buy you dinner.

FRAN. Dinner?

BRIAN. Do you like Italian?

FRAN. Italian.

BRIAN. Do you like movies?

FRAN. Movies. I love movies!

BRIAN. Fran!

FRAN. Yes!

BRIAN. We'll take in a movie!

FRAN. OK! (*They begin exiting rapidly arm in arm. He stops.*)

BRIAN. Fran!

FRAN. What!

BRIAN. Nothing. (*They exit. Silvio and Gately, U.L.*)

GATELY. Silvio.

SILVIO. Yeah Gately?

GATELY. Where do ducks go in the winter?

SILVIO. They fly south. They beat it on down to Florida. And places like that. They hang out. They get a tan.

GATELY. (*Nods.*) Think there's ducks in the park?

SILVIO. Yeah? You wanna see the ducks? You wanna feed the ducks? C'mon I'll buy a pretzel and we'll feed the ducks. (*Silvio takes him by the arm. They begin to head for the park. Gately stops.*)

GATELY. Boy. We got a helluva damn deal, didn't we.

SILVIO. (*Pause.*) Yeah. (*They exit U.L. Kevin and Sally, D.L. Mike with his back to audience, C. Kevin and Sally cross to R. Stop.*)

SALLY. Kev.

KEVIN. Yeah.

SALLY. Do you really love Rhoda?

KEVIN. Sal, we just needed time to think about it, and now that I've thought about it I don't need to think about it anymore.

SALLY. I love you Kev.

KEVIN. I love you Sally. (*They kiss.*) Hey Mikey! C'mon! We're gonna walk down Broadway. (*Mike runs over to them. Stops. Looks back at the Dakota.*)

MIKE. Yesterday . . . Everything was perfect. (*The three exit D.R. Music. Slow Blackout.*)

PROPERTY PLOT

PROP PRESET

ON STAGE

2 Trash cans—on spikes L. and R.
2 Park benches

R. PROP TABLE

Fold-up umbrella—Brian
Matches—Brian
Cigarette lighter—Brian
Gum—Wrigley's Spearmint—Brian
Cigarettes—Vantage—Brian

Men's handkerchief—Morris
Cane—Morris
Long umbrella—Fran
Fran's bag with:
    Chopsticks—3
    1 Chinese food container with popcorn—container in
    paper bag
    Cigarettes—Vantage
    Gum

Mikey's bag with:
  Matches
  Can of Coke
  NY Post (Sports section)
  Gum
  Fig Newtons

Sally's bag with:
  Oreos
  Red purse with:
    3 joints
  "We remember" sign — folded as per actress' request
  Handkerchief (Kleenex)
  Hairpin

Matches — Kevin
Gum — Kevin

L. PROP TABLE

Cigarettes — Marlboros — Silvio
Matches — Silvio
Wallet with 67 dollars — Silvio
Soft pretzel — Silvio

Pack of Lifesavers — Larry
"Ghettoblaster"(radio) — Larry

New TITLES

FOOL FOR LOVE
DOG EAT DOG
MR. & MRS.
A PLACE ON THE MAGDALENA FLATS
COURTSHIP
MY UNCLE SAM
GREAT EXPECTATIONS
THREE SISTERS
TWAIN PLUS TWAIN
LAUGHING STOCK
BONJOUR LA BONJOUR
THE OMELET MURDER CASE

● *Write for Information*

DRAMATISTS PLAY SERVICE, INC.
440 Park Avenue South   New York, N.Y. 10016

New  PLAYS

BABY WITH THE BATHWATER

THE LADY AND THE CLARINET

THE VAMPIRES

THE BEARD

LUNATIC AND LOVER

LITTLE BIRD

THE WHALES OF AUGUST

THE FATHER

THE SOUND OF A VOICE

POTHOLES

LES BELLES SOEURS

LITTLE VICTORIES

INQUIRIES INVITED

 DRAMATISTS PLAY SERVICE, INC.
440 Park Avenue South   New York, N. Y. 10016